Alcohol and You

Also by Essie E. Lee

CAREERS IN THE HEALTH FIELD

Also by Elaine Israel

THE GREAT ENERGY SEARCH

Alcohol and You

By ESSIE E. LEE
and ELAINE ISRAEL

Illustrated by
Jerry Smath

JULIAN MESSNER NEW YORK

Published by Julian Messner, a Division of Simon & Schuster, Inc.
A Gulf + Western Company
1 West 39 Street, New York, N.Y. 10018.

Printed in the United States of America

Design by Marjorie Zaum

Second Printing, 1976

Library of Congress Cataloging in Publication Data

Lee, Essie E.

Alcohol and you.

SUMMARY: Explores the origins and uses of alcohol, its effect on the body, and the physical and social problems it can cause.

1. Alcoholism—Juvenile literature. 2. Alcohol—Physiological effect—Juvenile literature. 4. Alcoholism—Treatment—Juvenile literature. [1. Alcohol. 2. Alcoholism] I. Israel, Elaine, joint author.

II. Title.

HV5066.L43 362.2'92 75-29429
ISBN 0-671-32758-5
ISBN 0-671-32759-3 lib. bdg.

Contents

Alcohol and You

When Two Drinks Are Too Many 1

When twelve-year-old Mark invited Brian and Jennifer to spend the day at his house, it sounded great. Mark had said, "My folks won't be home. We can play records."

Being alone in the house and playing the stereo as loud as they wanted had been okay for a while. But then they got bored.

Mark said, "Hey, want a drink? A real drink? Not soda pop. It's fun."

Brian and Jennifer hesitated.

"Don't be babies," coaxed Mark. "We'll just have one drink. It's no big thing. I have it all the time."

"Oh, all right," said Brian, secretly curious to know how liquor tasted.

"Just one," said Jennifer, still not too sure.

They gulped the whiskey down as if it were

medicine. The flavor was strange. And it burned—they felt it going down all the way to their stomachs. It made them feel peculiar—floating, giggly.

Before they knew it, Mark was saying, "How about another one?"

Several drinks later, Jennifer lay on the living room floor. This time she hadn't made it to the bathroom to vomit.

Brian's head hung between his legs. Just a minute before he'd felt like floating. But now, he was sick to his stomach, fainting, and scared.

Mark was laughing and crying at the same time. He couldn't make the bottle cap fit on the bottle.

Mark, Brian, and Jennifer were drunk.

When they were sober, Brian and Jennifer wondered why drinking had seemed such a special, fun thing to do.

Drinking was a new experience for them. The year before, drinking had been a new experience for Mark, too. But now he was hooked—hooked on the world's oldest drug: alcohol.

Mark and millions more are part of the long and stormy history of alcoholic beverages.

2 A Long and Stormy History

Divers recently discovered a sunken ship dating back over 5,000 years to the Bronze Age. Among the things they found was a bronze wine pitcher. From discoveries like these, we know that alcoholic beverages have been used since pre-historic times. Probably some caveman accidentally discovered that, in warm weather, fruit juices changed into a pleasant tasting beverage that did strange things to him when he drank it.

We know that in Biblical times, wine was an important beverage. The story of Noah tells how he left the ark, found some dry land, and planted a vineyard. It also tells how he became drunk on the wine from its grapes!

Wine has been used as part of religious ceremonies since ancient times. Many Jewish people serve specially blessed wine at weddings, confirma-

tions, and the Sabbath dinner. The Roman Catholics use wine to celebrate mass. During the Middle Ages, monks made the wine in their monasteries. Their recipes were carefully guarded secrets. Other Christian religions use wine at their services. Some other religions, like Mohammedanism, forbid the use of alcoholic beverages at any time.

Alcohol as a beverage has played an important part in American history, too. The Pilgrim leader, William Bradford, decided that the *Mayflower* should land at Plymouth Rock because "We could not take much time for further search and consideration, our victuals being much spent, especially beer."

Beer—and, later, rum—were popular beverages among the colonists. But those who drank too much of them were considered sinful and weak. In 1619, the Virginia colony passed a law against drinking too much. For a short time, liquor was banned in the colony of Georgia. In New England, drunkards were punished in public. They were flogged, put into stocks, or forced to wear a large letter "D" around their necks.

In colonial days, beer was a table drink. Sometimes it was even given to children, if water was unfit to drink. During the American Revolution, soldiers and sailors were given a rum ration. The drink was thought to be good for their health. So making beer, wines, and liquors became thriving businesses.

After the Revolution, when money was needed to run the new nation, the government taxed alcoholic beverages. Americans didn't like being taxed by their own government any more than they had liked being taxed by Britain. To dodge the tax, some colonists moved westward into the Ohio Valley.

Farmers in Pennsylvania rioted and chased the tax collectors from their farms. Troops were sent in, and the resistance was put down. The farmers lost this Whiskey Rebellion. And the federal government proved its right to collect taxes and enforce the national laws.

Trade in *rum* and in *molasses*, which was used to make rum, was important in the economy of the new nation. The rum was traded for slaves in Africa. The slaves were taken to the West Indies, where they were traded for molasses. And then rum and molasses were traded for more slaves.

As settlers moved west, liquor went with them. Whiskey was one of the items they used to trade with the Indians for furs and lands.

By the middle 1800s, many groups felt there was too much drinking in the country. They formed temperance societies to convince people to stop drinking. Temperance workers held rallies, carried signs, and made speeches. Saloons, places which sold alcoholic beverages, were their special target. Saloons, they said, led customers to the devil. Carry Nation, a member of the Women's Christian

Temperance Union, went into some saloons with ax in hand, and chopped them up. She was arrested many times, but jail sentences did not stop her!

At the same time the Anti-Saloon League was working in more legal ways to make America "dry." The League wanted laws passed to stop all drinking of liquor. It gave its money and votes to those political candidates who promised to get prohibition laws passed.

In time, these anti-alcohol groups grew into a national political party, the Prohibition Party. And they achieved their goal. On January 16, 1920, the 18th Amendment to the Constitution went into effect. The sale or manufacture of alcohol for drinking was illegal. The law limited the amount of alcohol in a beverage to one-half of one per cent. The sale and use of alcohol in medicine and industry were not stopped.

The Prohibition Era had begun. It was called the "noble experiment," because it was intended to help people. The experiment failed, though. It failed because many people broke the law. They felt they had the right to decide for themselves whether or not to drink.

They went to *speakeasies* (secret saloons) to drink. They bought liquor from *bootleggers* who smuggled in liquor from other countries. Liquor,

sometimes poisonous, was even bought from people who made it in their homes—"bathtub gin."

Owners of speakeasies, as well as bootleggers and makers of bathtub gin, grew rich. Gangs of criminals moved in on these money-making operations. Gangs warred among themselves for control of speakeasies and breweries. Trucks carrying liquor were hijacked. In some cities, there were street shootings. Gangs even began to control legal businesses. They also tried to influence people in government. The nation was terrorized.

Because of the rise in crimes, and because most people no longer wanted the prohibition amendment, it was repealed in 1933. But some states decided to keep prohibition. It did not end in Oklahoma until 1959. In Mississippi, the last state to repeal prohibition, it continued up to 1966.

The end of national prohibition did not mean the end of restrictions, however. Each state and some local communities passed their own laws for the sale and use of alcoholic beverages.

Merchants must get a license to sell alcoholic beverages. And they are charged a tax on every bottle they sell. A few states have state-managed stores, and liquor can be bought only in those places. In some states, the sale of liquor is forbidden on Sundays and on election days.

All states have age restrictions on drinking.

20 In 17 states, a person cannot be served alcoholic beverages in a public place until the age of 18. Twenty-seven other states have set the age at 21.

Why do the states have such different laws relating to alcoholic beverages? It is mostly because the people who live in each state have different ideas on the subject.

But most people do not *really* know much about alcohol. They need to find out, so they can make intelligent decisions vital to themselves, to their families, and to their communities.

3

What Is Alcohol?

There are many kinds of alcohol.

Most are used for commercial and industrial purposes. These are made from oil and petroleum products, and are deadly poisons if swallowed. Three that you and your family probably use are methyl alcohol, denatured alcohol, and isopropyl alcohol.

Methyl alcohol is used in hundreds of products, including paint and cleaning solutions, and as antifreeze. Water in the radiator is usually enough to cool the working engine of a car. But it freezes when the temperature goes down to 32° F. (0° C). The freezing temperature of methyl alcohol is much lower. Therefore, when it is added to the radiator, the danger of water freezing is lessened.

Denatured alcohol is alcohol to which a definite amount of poisonous alcohol has been added to make it undrinkable. This is allowed under strict government regulations. Denatured alcohol is good for cleaning skin, and helps prevent infections from wounds. It is also used for antifreeze and fuels.

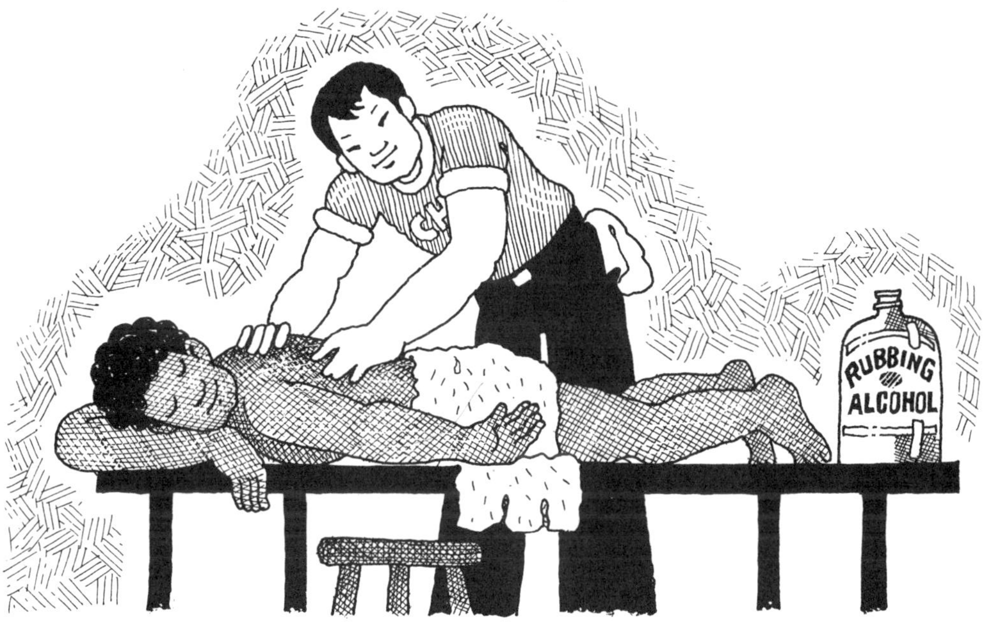

Isopropyl alcohol is often used in rubbing alcohol. It cools the skin, and helps relieve muscle pains. Doctors sometimes recommend rubbing alcohol to bring down high fevers, or for relieving sore muscles. Shaving lotion, hair tonic, perfume, and iodine contain isopropyl.

Commercial and industrial alcohols are important to the business life of our country. They are not meant for drinking. But unfortunately, sometimes people do drink them. A small item tucked away in the back pages of a city newspaper recently read:

> Two men died early yesterday after drinking methyl alcohol. A third man is in serious condition. He was delirious when brought to the hospital. He is now partly blind. The men drank the poisonous alcohol because they could not afford beverage alcohol.

Beverage alcohol is *ethyl alcohol* mixed with water and other liquids to make it safe to drink. Pure ethyl alcohol is poisonous. It is used in its pure form in antifreeze, solvents, and rubbing alcohols.

Ethyl alcohol is made by fermenting grains (such as barley, rye, corn, wheat), or fruits (such as grapes, berries, apples, plums), or potatoes. Fermentation is a process of nature.

Did you ever leave a container of milk on the table over night? Did the smell and taste change? If they did, *fermentation* took place. Tiny yeast plants, too small to be seen, float in the air all the time. When they land in a warm liquid like milk, they work on the sugars in it. The sweet milk is turned sour. The same kind of fermentation process is used to make wine and beer.

Winemakers add yeast to the warm juices or syrups of grapes, berries, or other fruit. The yeast works on the sugar in the juice or syrup, changing it to alcohol and a gas—carbon dioxide. The gas is allowed to escape into the air. Fermentation goes on until all the sugar has been changed. Then the process stops, leaving the wine with up to 12% alcoholic content. But winemakers sometimes add extra ethyl alcohol to make a stronger drink.

Brewers make beer from grains, most often barley, mixed with corn or rice and hops. The grains go though a "malting" process to change the starch in them to sugar. Yeast changes the sugar to ethyl alcohol. *Hops* are added to give beer its special flavor. When the fermentation stops, the alcohol content of beer ranges from 3% to 6%.

Stronger alcoholic beverages are made by the process of *distillation*. Fermented wines and cereals are boiled. The rising steam from the boiling process contains most of the alcohol. This steam is collected and cooled. The result is a liquid with a high ethyl alcohol content—whiskey, rum, vodka, gin, brandy, and others. *Tequila*, a favorite Mexican drink, is made by distilling the fermented juice of the century plant.

4 Drinking and Getting Drunk

Ethyl alcohol—usually called alcohol—is both a food and a drug.

Food is needed for health, growth, and energy. Since ethyl alcohol is a food, you might think it has to be good for you. Wrong! It is a food with no nutritional value. Unlike foods such as fish, meat, eggs, vegetables, and cereals, alcohol con-

tains no proteins, vitamins, or minerals. It just has fattening calories.

Alcohol is the most widely used drug in the world. And like all drugs, alcohol causes changes in the body. Some can be helpful. Doctors sometimes suggest alcohol for certain patients. A small amount of whiskey can improve sluggish circulation. Or a little wine is used to stimulate the appetite.

For most adults, whose systems can handle alcohol, small amounts on social occasions can be pleasant. A glass of wine or beer can make a good meal taste even better. A drink and some food with friends can be relaxing.

But alcohol as a drug can have harmful effects, too. One of the most familiar is *drunkenness*—the abuse of alcohol.

Not everyone gets drunk after a drink or two. But even after one drink, slight changes do occur in the body.

After two or three drinks, drunkenness, or *intoxication*, can set in. The alcohol gets to the brain and slows it down. Thinking, moving, remembering become difficult. The person begins to lose control over coordination. Walking becomes unsteady because balance and coordination are af-

fected. Putting one foot in front of the other to walk a straight line becomes difficult. The person may stagger and sway.

After three or four drinks, a drinker may feel able to do anything—silly things like dancing on a table, or something even dangerous like walking on a high ledge. The part of the brain that would usually say, "Don't do it," is not performing its job. Sometimes, a quiet, gentle person becomes a "roaring lion" under the influence of alcohol.

A person who has drunk a lot of alcohol also gradually loses control over speech. "She sells sea-shells by the seashore" becomes really hard to say.

For a driver who has had too much liquor, judging distances becomes harder. Reaction time is slowed down so it takes longer to put a foot on the brake. Vision is blurred so that road signs appear fuzzy. Hearing is dulled. The drunken driver causes a high rate of accidents.

Can you see why people are warned not to drive if they have been drinking?

When the alcoholic content of the blood reaches .05%, a person is considered, in some states, to be drunk. With this much alcohol in the blood, most drivers have slower *reflexes*, and so are no longer safe drivers.

To test the amount of alcohol in the blood, most police use a *Breathalyzer*. When a person blows into this device, any alcohol on the breath mixes with the chemicals in the Breathalyzer, and changes them. These changes are recorded in percentage amounts on a dial. And the drivers whose percentage is greater than the law allows, soon find themselves jailed and fined for Driving While Intoxicated (DWI).

Each person has his or her own *tolerance* for alcohol. It can vary from day to day. Tolerance also depends on the size of the drinker, and how and when the drinking takes place.

A 200-pound person will not get drunk so fast as one weighing 75 pounds. Why? A larger person has more blood and body fluids to mix with the alcohol and dilute it. Therefore, the more diluted alcohol has less effect on the body.

Does alcohol remain in the body forever? No. Much of it is oxidized (combined with oxygen and burned) in the liver. The rest of the alcohol leaves the body in urine, as perspiration, and on the breath. Have you ever been near a drinker? You can smell the alcohol on his breath.

Some drinkers believe that drinking coffee, taking a cold shower or a long walk will help a person to become *sober* quickly—that is, to get rid of the alcohol faster. But these so-called cures do not help. The body takes its own time to eliminate the alcohol. And the length of time differs with each person.

After sobering up, sometimes a person has a hangover. A *hangover* is a series of reactions of the body. These reactions may include vomiting, dizziness, a headache, anxiety or fatigue.

All these effects on the body are temporary, if the drinker can stop drinking long enough to give the body time to eliminate the alcohol in the blood. But many persons become so dependent on alcohol that they cannot stop. Such persons are alcoholics. They may be seriously harmed by, or die from, the more dangerous effects of addiction to alcohol.

Other Effects of Alcohol on the Body

5

When alcohol enters the body, it goes immediately to the stomach and the small intestine. Unlike other foods, it does not start being digested there. Instead, it goes undigested into the bloodstream. Then the bloodstream, pumped by the heart, carries the alcohol to all parts of the body.

The heart, and the veins and arteries of the bloodstream, can be harmed by alcohol. The heart beats faster, which is especially dangerous for people with heart problems. The walls of the arteries can thicken, making it harder for blood to get through. This forces the blood pressure higher. And if there is not enough blood supplied to any part of the body, that part is damaged beyond repair.

Some heavy drinkers develop a skin condition called *acne rosacea* (ro-za-see-a). The blood vessels

Schematic of Body Areas Affected by Alcohol

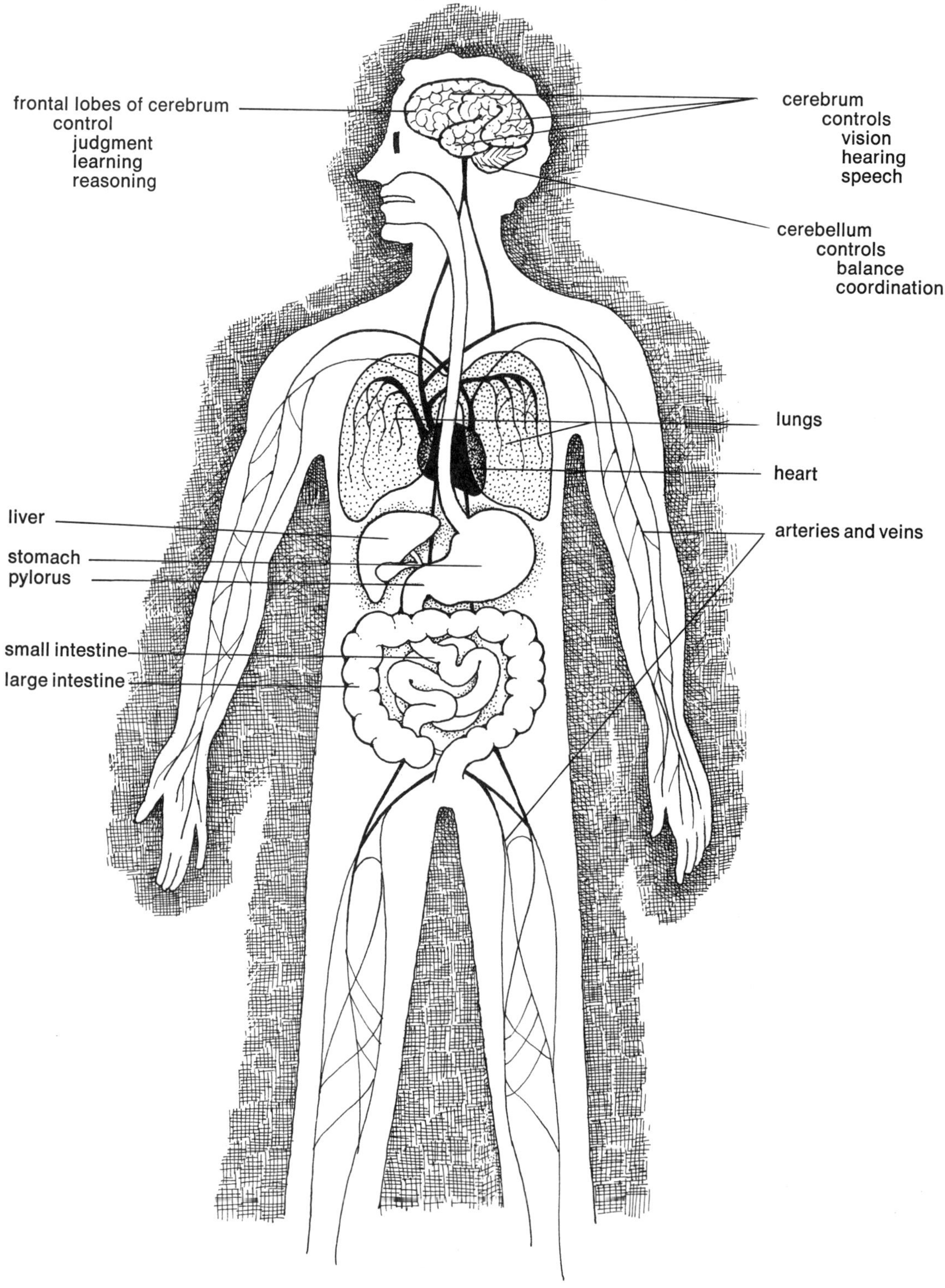

in the face redden and get bigger, particularly on the nose.

Very heavy drinking can injure the brain, and lead to mental illness, paralysis, speech problems, coma, or death. It can cause *delirium tremens* (the DTs). The sufferer hallucinates: hears and sees hideous things no one else can hear or see. Snakes, huge bugs, horrible monsters, and other things that aren't there at all seem to be attacking and crawling over the body. Often the victim tries to commit suicide to get away from these hallucinations.

The DTs are really a kind of *withdrawal* reaction—the body's way of protesting that it is not getting the alcohol it is used to. The DTs are quite similar to the withdrawal reactions of an *addict.*

Other parts of the body can also be damaged by the abuse of alcohol. The lining of the stomach can become painfully inflamed. The kidneys can become diseased and fail, causing death. When the alcohol reaches the liver, it becomes swollen and sensitive. And it can result in a disease called *cirrhosis* (sir-oh-sis) of the liver, which is often fatal.

Heavy drinkers have other kinds of health problems, too. Very often they do not eat properly, and so do not get enough iron and other nutrients.

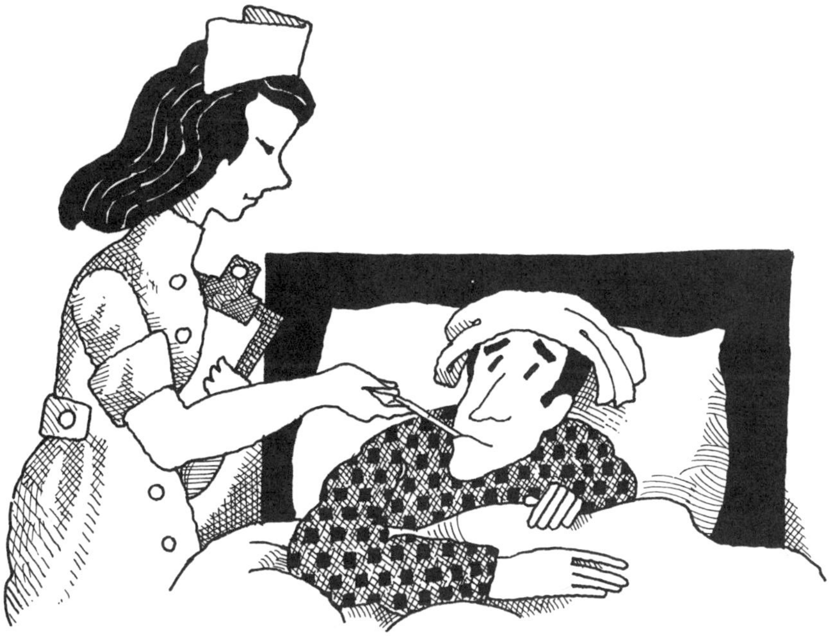

They can become too weak to function properly. They cannot fight off illnesses and other infections. And they often get pneumonia or tuberculosis.

Sometimes the body does protect itself. The *pylorus*, the lower end of the stomach that connects with the intestines, comes to the rescue—although it may not seem like that when it happens.

The pylorus opens and closes periodically to let partially-digested food enter the small intestine. Sometimes when a person drinks too much alcohol, the pylorus closes tight. Then the alcohol can't get into the intestine and stays in the stomach. But the pylorus charges for this service: When it locks, the drinker becomes nauseous and vomits. However, drinkers who have become accustomed to alcohol lose this protection.

Alcoholics and Alcoholism 6

Alcoholism is a disease. *Alcoholics* are people who can't get through the day without a drink. They let alcohol control their lives.

Alcoholism does not strike overnight. It works slowly, sneaking up on a person. Its victims usually don't know they've been caught until it is too late.

Most people think of an alcoholic as the scruffy bum, begging for money or lying drunk in a doorway with an empty bottle nearby. The bum may be an alcoholic. But 95% of all alcoholics are far from being bums. They are doctors, lawyers, students, plumbers, police officers, housewives. They are rich and poor, all ages, all religions, races, and nationalities. And more and more are young people like Jimmy.

Jimmy's parents gave him sips of their drinks from the time he was very young. He got to like the taste. As he grew older, he would sneak a drink. By the time he was 9, Jimmy found it hard to make it through the school day without a drink. So he would add a shot of whiskey to the milk in his thermos. At the age of 9, Jimmy had become an alcoholic.

Today, there is a rise in alcoholism among teenagers and even subteens. There are various causes for it.

Some young people drink to escape their problems. For a short time, while they drink, they feel better. Maybe they think they're "with it," that it is an adult thing to do. Maybe it seems daring because alcohol is usually forbidden. And maybe young people, like older drinkers, drink because for a while they feel more sure of themselves. They're less afraid of meeting people, of taking tests, facing problems, and becoming bored.

Being around people who drink leads some people to alcohol—and to becoming alcoholics. "I wanted to be one of the gang," says Donna. "So I started drinking with older kids who were always drinking. I was 11 years old when I started. Now I'm 15 and stuck with a drinking problem I'm trying to kick."

Some are switching from other drugs to alcohol. Alcohol is cheaper and easier to buy. And most young drinkers don't realize alcohol can be as dangerous as hard drugs.

For many years, alcoholics were treated as

drunks who could stop their drinking "if they really wanted to." Today, people who are studying alcoholism, know this is not so. Alcoholics find it hard to stop drinking even though they know it is slowly killing them.

Authorities do not agree on the causes of alcoholism. Some say there is a still-unknown chemical imbalance in the body that causes alcoholism. Others say it is an allergic reaction. Still others say it is a psychological disorder. Many feel that alcoholism may result from a combination of these physical and emotional causes.

Research also shows that children's surroundings and experiences may be responsible for their becoming alcoholics. Many children imitate their parents. If parents drink a lot, a child may want to

do the same. On the other hand, it has been found that in homes where alcohol is strictly forbidden, children sometimes grow into abusers of alcohol.

Alcohol abuse has become the number one drug problem in the United States. The National Commission on Marijuana and Drug Abuse says that alcohol is "the most widely used mood altering drug."

Abuse of alcohol creates many problems. Industry and the government lose ten billion dollars a year because of employees who have drinking problems. Health and welfare expenses for heavy drinkers cost the nation about two billion dollars a year.

Countless lives are wasted. Every year, at least 28,000 deaths in car accidents can be blamed on a driver or pedestrian who drank too much. Half a million people are badly injured in traffic accidents caused by someone under the influence of alcohol. Many victims are children. And many of the drunken drivers are under 21 years of age.

Sam, now 15, remembers that "school was a hassle. So I got a friend to buy liquor for me. One morning I found myself in a police station. It seems my friend and I stole a car. I don't remember. We smashed it up. My friend was killed."

Half of the murders in the United States involve someone who was drinking alcohol. And one-fourth of the suicide victims are found to have large amounts of alcohol in their bodies.

The abuse of alcohol often leads to separation of families by desertion, divorce, and death. Jay, 11, can't wait to finish school so he can work. His older sister has already dropped out in order to find a job. Their father spent all his money on liquor, and then deserted them. There isn't enough money for rent and food. How will the family stay together?

Tina doesn't really want her family to stay together. Often when she comes home from school, she finds her little brother has been badly beaten by her mother. Many child beaters are alcoholics.

Alcoholism doesn't only affect the drinker. It hurts family, friends, co-workers—everyone.

7 Getting Help

What can be done to help the alcoholic?

Before they're hooked, people can be educated to understand what alcoholism is and what it does. They can learn to handle themselves and liquor intelligently. They can learn how much, when and where to drink. They can learn to feel good about themselves—without the help of drugs such as alcohol.

After they're hooked, it's not very easy.

Robin B. and her mother live in a small apartment in Chicago. This is the fifth home they've had since Robin's parents were divorced. That was four years ago, when Robin was eight.

All her life, Mrs. B. drank. She couldn't hold a job because she was often drunk by the time she got to work. Or she'd drink during lunch and not make it back to the office.

No job meant no money. So every time their landlord insisted on the rent, Robin and her mother would move out in the middle of the night.

Robin was getting more and more scared. When she said something about not drinking anymore, her mother would scream, "I can stop drinking anytime I want to. I can, I can."

But she didn't, because she couldn't. She, too, felt alone and helpless.

Then, one afternoon, Mrs. B. "blacked out." Robin found her on the kitchen floor. Mrs. B. couldn't remember what had happened or how she had gotten there. After that, she decided to find help. She knew she was sick.

She began going to meetings of *Alcoholics Anonymous* (AA). There she met other alcoholics.

They talked openly about their problems. Mrs. B. chose a partner to whom she could turn for help whenever she felt the urge to drink. Both she and her partner were trying to help themselves and each other live from one day to the next without taking a drink. Just one day at a time. The AA meetings opened with the prayer:

> God grant me the Serenity to accept the things I cannot change; the Courage to change the things I can, and the Wisdom to know the difference.

At the same time, Robin went to *ALATEEN*, the group for children of alcoholics. There she met other young people with whom she could share her troubles. At ALATEEN meetings, Robin learned that alcoholism is an illness that can be treated. She learned never to make her mother feel guilty about being an alcoholic. She learned to make her mother feel good about herself. Robin let her mother know over and over again that she was loved and needed. And Robin learned that she herself shouldn't feel responsible for her mother's illness.

ALATEEN
MEET HERE FOR RAP SESSIONS
WEDNESDAY NIGHTS

That was two years ago. Mrs. B. hasn't had a drink since. But she didn't pledge never to drink again. At Alcoholics Anonymous she learned to say, "I will not drink today." She takes each day as it comes.

Mrs. B. and Robin are lucky to have each other. The two now have lots of good times together. They go shopping. They go bowling. They go bicycling. They talk to each other about their feelings and their ideas. It's good for Mrs. B., and it's good for Robin.

Alcoholics Anonymous is a national organization with branches all over the United States. Robin and Mrs. B.—and thousands of others—found help there. There are other places, too, to go for help.

Special hospitals have modern treatment programs for alcoholic patients. Two of these hospitals are Mount Zion in San Francisco, California, and Massachusetts General Hospital in Boston. Veterans can be helped in hospitals run by the Veterans Administration in all states.

Community mental health centers often treat drinkers. Some centers are open 24 hours a day for help. Their addresses are in the phone book.

The National Council on Alcoholism, 733 Third Avenue, New York, N.Y. 10016, has lists of helping groups across the United States.

For information on alcoholism write to the National Clearinghouse for Alcohol Information, Box 2345, Rockville, Maryland 20852.

The school guidance counselor, a religious leader, and neighborhood agencies often can provide help, or tell where it can be found.

A well-known doctor says:

> Drinking in itself is not wrong. What's terribly important is knowing when to stop and being strong enough to do it. Drinking often starts out as being fun and games. Few people believe it can end in death, as it sometimes does. Drinking is like an elevator that only goes in one direction: DOWN. When you get off is up to you.

One day, for one reason or another, you may have to decide whether to drink or not. It's good to know the facts. They will help you to make responsible decisions about alcohol and you.

Glossary

ABUSE: To take a drug for any purpose not intended by the manufacturer of the drug. Abuse of a drug can result in injury to the body.

ACNE ROSACEA: A skin disease in which the face becomes red, especially around the nose, and the eyes become very red—"bloodshot." Too much alcohol in the blood is the cause.

ADDICT: Anyone who is dependent upon alcohol or other drugs, and who would suffer withdrawal disorders if the drug were taken away.

ALATEEN: A group of children of alcoholics who learn how to help themselves, and deal with their families.

ALCOHOL: Any one of several kinds of colorless, flammable liquids, with a pleasant odor and a very sharp, burning taste. One kind—ethyl alcohol, is both a food and a drug. *See also* methyl alcohol; alcoholic beverage; denatured alcohol; isopropyl.

ALCOHOLIC: An addict who is dependent upon alcohol. See addict.

ALCOHOLIC BEVERAGE: Any drink that contains at least two per cent alcohol by volume. Beer has the least amount of alcohol, 3 to 6 per cent; absinthe, a strong bitter drink, has the most—68 per cent.

ALCOHOLICS ANONYMOUS (AA): A worldwide, nonprofit organization, founded in 1935, to help people who want to stop drinking alcoholic beverages.

BEER: An alcoholic beverage made by fermenting and brewing grains such as barley, mixed with either corn or rice, and flavored with hops. Beer contains from 3 to 6 per cent alcohol.

BOOTLEGGER: A person who transports or sells liquor illegally.

BRAIN: The master organ that controls the body. Too much liquor can result in a temporary disorder of the brain known as drunkenness.

BRANDY: An alcoholic beverage made by distillation of fruits such as peaches, grapes, apples, and plums. *See* distillation.

BREATHALYZER: Machine for measuring alcohol content of the body.

CIRRHOSIS: A disease that occurs most often in the kidneys and the liver. It is a hardening and scarring of the organ. Heavy drinkers are often victims of cirrhosis, especially cirrhosis of the liver.

COMA: The state of complete loss of consciousness. The form of coma most often seen is that which results when a person becomes so drunk that the brain loses control over much of the body.

COORDINATION: The working together of various muscles to produce a certain movement.

DELIRIUM TREMENS (DTs): A serious disorder of the mind and body. It lasts from two to ten days. Its effects include seeing things that are not there—unreal things, called hallucinations. It is one of the results of alcoholism.

DENATURED ALCOHOL: Ethyl alcohol to which methyl alcohol has been added in exact amounts so as to make the alcohol a poison. The purpose is to stop human beings from using it as a beverage. However, some alcoholics will drink denatured alcohol, and many die from it.

DISTILLATION: Heating a liquid until it becomes a steam or vapor, and then letting it cool to form a liquid again. It is a way of making liquors such as whiskey and brandy.

DRUG: Any solid, liquid or gas used in medicine for the treatment of diseases or disorders. All drugs are designed to make people feel better or to improve their health but they are not always used that way.

DRUNKENNESS: The temporary loss of control over part of the body because of taking in too much alcohol.

ETHYL ALCOHOL: The best known of all the kinds of alcohol, it is also known as grain alcohol. It is the only kind that can be drunk in small amounts without killing the drinker.

FERMENTATION: The chemical changes that happen to fruit sugar which turn it into alcohol. The changes are caused by tiny living things such as yeast, molds or bacteria germs. Wine and beer are made by fermentation.

HANGOVER: The tired, aching, and sometimes sick feeling that is caused by the drinking of too much alcoholic beverages. A hangover appears after a person has become sober.

HOPS: A vine-like plant whose flowers are used to give a flavor to beer.

HEART: The organ that keeps the blood circulating in the body. It works like a pump, and does not stop from birth until death.

INTOXICATION: See drunkenness.

ISOPROPYL ALCOHOL: A clear, flammable liquid, similar to ethyl alcohol, but taken in any amount, it can kill the drinker. It is best known for its use in rubbing alcohol.

KIDNEYS: A pair of bean-shaped organs that separate and take out liquid wastes of the body and excrete it as urine.

LIQUOR: Any distilled alcoholic beverage. *See* distillation.

LIVER: A large organ that helps in the digestion of food, in supplying sugar to the body, in regulating the clotting of blood, and in producing antibodies which prevent disease. *See* cirrhosis.

METHYL ALCOHOL: A colorless, flammable liquid that is also known as wood alcohol or methanol. It is a poison, used mostly in automobile antifreeze, and in paints and cleaners. Methyl alcohol can never be made drinkable.

MOLASSES: A thick, dark-colored syrup that forms as a waste in the making of sugar from sugarcane. Rum is made from molasses.

PROHIBITION: Forbidding the sale, manufacture or transporting of alcoholic beverages. Prohibition became the policy of the United States government from 1920 to 1933, and prohibition remained the policy of some of the states until 1966.

PYLORUS: A ringlike set of muscles in the bottom of the stomach. It keeps food in the stomach until the food becomes liquified and ready to move into the intestines.

REFLEX: Any movement that occurs in some part of the body without thought or effort. For example, the movement that happens when the fingers touch a hot stove is a reflex.

RUM: An alcoholic beverage distilled from molasses. See molasses.

SOBER: Not under the influence of alcohol—not drunk.

SOCIAL DRINKER: A person who drinks alcoholic beverages in the company of others, usually as an act of friendship, or to be "social."

SPEAKEASY: A place where alcoholic beverages are sold illegally. Many speakeasies existed in the United States during the era of prohibition that lasted from 1920 to 1933.

STOMACH: An organ of digestion and for storing food during the digesting process.

TEQUILA: A fermented beverage made from the juice of the agave, or century, plant.

TOLERANCE: The power of resisting the actions of a drug.

WHISKEY: A distilled liquor, made from grain—usually rye, barley or corn. The word whisky, without the "e," refers to a kind of liquor made in Canada or Scotland, and is also known as "scotch."

WINE: An alcoholic beverage made from the fermented juice of grapes or other fruits. It differs from brandy because it is made by the process of fermentation, while brandy is made by distillation. See fermentation; distillation.

Index